Jre



Arnold R. Hofer

# WHAT DOES IT MEAN TO BE *Born Again?*

JOHN L VIGNES

ISBN: 978-0-578-29946-4 (Paperback edition)



Graphic Design and Formatting by Tami Boyce Design
(tamiboyce.com)

# DISCLAIMER

The author has done his best to interpret scripture correctly. This book contains my interpretations, views, thoughts, words, and experience. They are mine. You may differ from me in your interpretations, views, thoughts, words, and experiences. Any statement cannot take the place of your own ability to evaluate scripture or the words in this book and make your own decisions.

The author will not be held liable or responsible for any misunderstanding or misuse of any information in this book. The author is not responsible for any loss, damage, or injury caused or alleged to be caused by information in this book.

The author hopes you find this book useful. The effects of carrying out any of the ideas in this book will vary from person to person. There is no guarantee of any outcome by applying any of the principles in this book.

# DEDICATION

**I would like to dedicate this book to Jon Knochenmus: my friend, my business partner, and my brother in Christ.** Jon is an owner of Ralco in Marshall, Minnesota. At one time Jon left Ralco and worked at the same company as me. Jon told me when he started that one day he would go back to Ralco, and he did.

In 1983 I created The Genesis Diet (Genesis). It was a high nutrient dense milk pellet for baby pigs. A small amount of Genesis was fed right after weaning and we got a tremendous result. It was the first feed over $1,000 per ton in the swine industry. At first, we were very successful, but soon competitors copied us. They would sell their knock off products by saying "This is just like Genesis, only cheaper." Since Genesis was the most expensive product on the market and we only had one product, the company failed. I had no ownership in Genesis, I was the nutritionist.

Not only did I lose my job, but my wife lost her job at the same time. I had a wife, two small children, AND NO INCOME. I went through five hard years of severe financial difficulty. We almost lost our home. I was very hurt by what happened to me in the feed industry. I had created a tremendous product. Now everyone copied me and were making money off my idea. I was determined to never work in the feed industry again.

During these five hard years I did as the Bible says, "Whatever your hand finds to do, do it with all your might..." That's what I did. Somehow, with God's help, we made it. During this time, I got closer to God and stronger in my faith. I always tithed during this hard time (gave 10% of my income to God).

Jon was always there, giving me constant encouragement. He kept trying to hire me as a salesman for Ralco. I said "Jon, I am a nutritionist and not a salesman." In May 1994 Jon called me. He said, I've been praying and God wants to get you back in the feed industry." I almost laughed at him like Sarah did in the Bible. God told Sarah she would have a child when she was beyond child bearing age and she laughed. I felt like laughing at Jon, but I agreed to meet with him.

We met at the Prairie House Restaurant in Gaylord, Minnesota in May 1994. Jon asked me,

"What would it take to get you back in the feed industry?" I told him I wanted to own my own business and he worked it out. **Remember, I had no money.** My company (Advanced Birthright Nutrition) was born. **God gave me inspiration and I created Birthright Baby Pig Milk Replacer.** Ralco gave me a monthly draw (it had to be paid back), manufactured, sold, and shipped Birthright. I gave Ralco the world-wide rights to market Birthright. Ralco gave me a commission for the Birthright that was sold.

We started selling Birthright in June 1994. When I started my business, I had a car with 200,000 miles on it, a hole in the floor, and a door falling off. During the first three months, Jon set all my appointments. He drove me to every meeting. He paid for all my meals. He shared his hotel room with me. **What a friend! What a brother in Christ!** Now Birthright is sold all over the world. **I am biased, but I believe Birthright is the best milk replacer in the world.** God has prospered both of our companies—Ralco and Advanced Birthright Nutrition. **Thank you God and thank you Jon Knochenmus.** For your animal nutrition needs go to **www.ralco.com.**

# ACKNOWLEDGEMENTS

My wife Julia (Ronxin Xu) strongly encouraged me to write this book, gave me many good ideas and was with me every step of the way. **The first publisher that I submitted my manuscript to turned me down.** I went to my good friends (Jon Knochenmus, John Liston, and Mark Swanson) and my family—Kirsten Vignes (daughter) and Justin Vignes (son). As we discussed my book, they gave me many good ideas and constructive criticism. This greatly improved my book. Thank you all.

# FIRST REVIEWS

I really enjoyed your book. It was short and impactful. You explained things in a way most people will grasp.

It was excellent to add people who have used tracts to influence and convert others. I thought the call to action was a good idea as the book is not just to be read but also as a **tool that needs action through distribution.** I also like your final prayer asking God to use your book (What Does it Mean to Be Born Again?)

— ***Mark S. ( Massachusetts)***

I read your book. It was well written! Every point was easy to follow and you backed them with Words of the Bible. We think this book will be successful. The short length of the book also makes it an easier read.

— ***Susan and Larry F. (Minnesota)***

# ABOUT THE AUTHOR

JOHN L. VIGNES and his wife, Julia (Rongxin) live in Apple Valley, Minnesota. They have three grown children—Justin, Kirsten, and Mark (Shuaidong). John has an MS in Animal Science and owns his own business. John is also an Associate Pastor and an Evangelist. John's first book, *What Does it Mean to Be Born Again?*, was written with the strong encouragement of Julia. John has preached in and works with ministries in India. John actively reaches out to the world through his video sermons on Facebook and YouTube (John for Jesus).

IF THIS BOOK HAS IMPACTED YOU, PLEASE SHARE IT WITH US:
johnv@disciples.com

PURCHASE THE BOOK (WHAT DOES IT MEAN TO BE BORN AGAIN?) FROM AMAZON.

FOR GOOD PREACHING AND TEACHING ON THE CROSS I RECOMMEND:

**JOHN L VIGNES SERMONS**
Go to: www.youtube.com
Search: **JOHNLV John L Vignes Sermons**
Translations in: Hindi, Tamil, Telugu, Mandarin Chinese, Spanish

**SONLIFE TV**
www.sonlifetv.com
The Expositor's Study Bible
Jimmy Swaggart Bible Commentaries

**GOSPEL OF LIFE**
2010 Jefferson Road, Suite A
Northfield, Minnesota 55057
10:30 AM Sundays
www.gospeloflifechurch.org

# CONTENTS

# INTRODUCTION

Maybe you are not a Christian and someone asked you, "Have you been born again?" What does that mean? If you are a Christian, have you ever had the opportunity to share Jesus with someone and you talked about being born again and they absolutely could not understand what you were saying. Why couldn't they understand what you were saying? **What does it mean to be born again?**

## JESUS HAD AN ENCOUNTER LIKE THAT WITH NICODEMUS:

## JOHN 3:1-7

> 1 There was a man of the Pharisees, named Nicodemus, a Ruler of the Jews:

2 The same came to Jesus by night, and said unto Him, Rabbi, we know that You are a Teacher come from God: for no man can do these miracles that You do, except God be with Him.

3 Jesus answered and said unto him, verily, verily, I say unto you, **except a man be born again, he cannot see the Kingdom of God.**

4 Nicodemus said unto Him, **how can a man be born when he is old? Can he enter the second time into his mother's womb, and be born?**

5 Jesus answered, Verily, verily, I say unto you, **except a man be born of water and of the Spirit, he cannot enter into the Kingdom of God.**

6 That which is born of the flesh is flesh; and that which is born of the Spirit is spirit.

7 Marvel not that I said unto you, **you must be born again.**

Nicodemus was a ruler of the Jews. He was a very educated man. He went to the best seminaries or colleges of his day. He was taught the Old

Testament or the Law of Moses. **The Jews and his community would say he was one of the greatest Men of God of their day. They would have said Nicodemus was a very moral man.**

Yet, the first thing Jesus said to Nicodemus was "**Nicodemus you need to be born again**". Nicodemus could not understand this and said:

- **How can a man be born when he is old?**
- **Can he enter the second time into his mother's womb, and be born?**

Isn't that what many people say to us when we talk to them about being born again?

**My question to you is why couldn't Nicodemus understand what Jesus was saying?**

Why don't people understand what we are saying when we talk to them about being born again?

# SPIRIT, SOUL, AND BODY

**I am going to lay some ground work to answer this question.** At first you may not understand what I am writing, but when I get done sharing with you, you will clearly understand.

II CORINTHIANS 5:1

> For we know that if **our earthly house** of this Tabernacle were dissolved, we have a building of God, a house made not with hands, eternal in the Heavens.

**What is our earthly house?** If a married couple invited me to their house they would say "**John, come over to our house.**" Our is not the house. Our lives in the house, but our is not the house. **Our earthly house is our physical body.**

## II CORINTHIANS 4:16

> For which cause we faint not; but though our **outward man** perish, yet the **inward man** is renewed day by day.

**Who is the outward man?** It is our physical body. My outward man is perishing day by day. I have gold in my teeth. I have some problems with my knees. My hair has turned white. My outward man is perishing! **Who is the inward man?** Most say soul or spirit. My inward man is being renewed day by day!

## I THESSALONIANS 5:23

> And the very God of Peace Sanctify you wholly; and I pray God your whole **spirit and soul and body** be preserved blameless unto the coming of our Lord Jesus Christ.

It says **spirit, soul and body.** Notice there are three. It does not say spirit and body. It does not say soul and body. It says **spirit, soul, and body.** We know what the physical body is. What is the difference between the spirit and soul?

## HEBREWS 4:12

> For the Word of God is **quick**, and **powerful**, and **sharper** than any **two-edged sword**, piercing even to the dividing asunder of **soul and spirit, and of joints and marrow**, and is a discerner of the thoughts and intents of the heart.

It says **soul, spirit, joints and marrow.** Joints and marrow points to our physical body. All three are represented again—spirit, soul, and body. We know what our physical body is, but what is the difference between the spirit and soul? **The soul** is our mind. **The spirit** is our heart or inner most being.

I can prove you are a three part being—**spirit, soul, body.** Have you ever had a serious problem of some kind? **I had a serious financial problem once.** I lost my job and had two small children. It affected my physical body. I couldn't sleep. It affected my soul or mind. My mind was running every direction. I thought if I don't get a job, we will lose our house and be out in the street. However, in my heart, in my spirit, I knew somehow or some way, God would work it out for me—**and he did.** We are a three part being—**spirit, soul, and body.**

# WHAT DOES IT MEAN TO BE BORN AGAIN?

JOHN 4:24

**God is a Spirit**: and they who worship Him must worship Him in spirit and in truth.

Notice it does not say **that God is a great body.**

It does not say **God is a great mind or soul.**
It says **God is a Spirit.**

GENESIS 1:26

And God said, Let **Us** make man in our Image, and after our likeness..................

Us refers to the Trinity—the Father, the Son, and the Holy Spirit. **If I am made in the Image and**

**Likeness of God, and God is a Spirit, then what am I?** A spirit. The real John is a spirit. I have a mind (soul) and I live in a physical body, but the real John is a spirit.

GENESIS 2: 16-17

> [16] And the Lord God commanded the man, saying, of every tree of the Garden **you may freely eat:**
>
> [17] But of the Tree of the Knowledge of Good and Evil, you shall not eat of it: **for in the day that you eat thereof you shall surely die.**

We know that Adam and Eve sinned. We know Adam and Eve ate of the fruit God told them not to eat.

**When they ate of that fruit**, did their physical body die? **No! When they ate of the fruit**, did their soul or mind die? **No! When they ate of the fruit, THEIR SPIRIT DIED.** Their spirit was separated from God the Spirit. **That's what eternal death is.** Our spirit is separated from God the Spirit. Our spirit never really dies, but if you are not born again it is separated from God. **When you are born again, your spirit comes back into fellowship with God**

**the Spirit.** The spirit and soul are closely connected. When you physically die your spirit and soul will go to Heaven. In Heaven God will give you a new body (a Glorified Body).

**Didn't God give Adam and Eve a good deal?** The Garden of Eden was **Paradise.** Adam and Eve had everything they needed. They had a perfect environment or climate. They had fellowship with God. **God was their friend.**

**God only asked them not to do one thing, eat of that one tree.** What was the purpose of the tree? God gave man **a choice, to obey or not to obey.** God did not make us **robots**. God gave us **choice.**

**God gives each one of us a choice.** We don't have to be saved. We don't have to put our faith and trust in Jesus and what He did at the Cross. It is our choice. **It is the most important decision you will ever have to make.** It determines your eternal future. It determines whether **you will go to Heaven or hell.** You don't have to go to hell. It is your choice.

## FEED YOUR SPIRIT

MATTHEW 4:4

But He (**Jesus**) answered and said, It is written, **man shall not live by bread alone, but by every Word that proceeds out of the Mouth of God.**

Jesus had fasted **40 days** and then the devil came to tempt Jesus. The devil said, if you are the Son of God, turn these rocks into bread. Jesus said, "**Man shall not live by bread alone, but by every word that proceeds out of the Mouth of God.**" Jesus had fasted 40 days. If he did not feed his physical body, he would starve to death just like all of us.

**What man was Jesus speaking of that lives by every Word that comes out of the mouth of God?**

Your spirit. Your spirit lives on the Word of God. You feed your physical body food. You feed your soul or mind information. It is like a computer. You put information in and you get information out. You feed your spirit the Word of God.

**How many times do you feed your physical body every day?** Most people say they eat at least three times per day with snacks in between. **What if you fed your physical body only once a week?** Your physical body would look like a skeleton and eventually you might die.

Many Christians do not read their Bibles. They may go to church once a week where they may hear the Word of God, but they seldom read their Bible. To be honest, some churches are not preaching the Bible or the Word of God. **What do you think your spirit looks like if you only feed it once a week?** It will be weak and powerless. You must read your Bible every day to feed your spirit.

## THIS IS THE ADVICE GOD GAVE TO THE KINGS OF ISRAEL TO BE SUCCESSFUL

### DEUTERONOMY 17:18-20

18 And it shall be when he sits upon the throne
of his kingdom, that he shall write himself a

copy of this Law (The Bible at that time) in a book out of that which is before the Priests and Levites.

19 And it shall be with him, **and he shall read therein all the days of his life:** that he may learn to fear the Lord his God, **to keep all** the words of this Law and these Statutes, to do them.

20 That his heart may not be lifted up above his brethren, that he turn not aside from the commandment, to the right hand, or the left: to the end that he may prolong his days in his kingdom, he, and his children, in the midst of Israel.

God is basically saying to the kings of Israel, if you want to be a successful king, **you must feed your spirit the Word of God.** This is the best advice I could ever give to anyone. If you want to be successful in this life and eternity, **you must feed your spirit the Word of God.**

## THIS IS THE ADVICE GOD GAVE TO FAMILIES FOR SUCCESS

## DEUTERONOMY 11:18-21

18 Therefore shall **you lay up my words in your heart and soul,** and bind them for a sign upon your hand, that they may be as frontlets between your eyes.

19 And **you shall teach them your children,** speaking of them when you sit in your house, and when you walk by the way, when you lie down, and when you rise up.

20 And you shall write them upon the door posts of your house, and upon your gates:

21 That your days be multiplied, and the days of your children, in the land the Lord swore unto your fathers to give them, as the days of heaven upon your gates.

God is basically saying, if you want your family to be successful, **you must feed your family (their spirits), the Word of God.**

ROMANS 12:1

> I beseech you therefore, Brethren, by the Mercies of God, that **you present your bodies a Living Sacrifice,** holy, acceptable unto God, which is your reasonable service.

It says **You present your body.** Who is you? You is not the body, because you is presenting the body. **You is your Spirit.**

ROMANS 12:2

> And be not conformed to this world: **but be you transformed by the renewing of your mind (soul)**, that you may prove what is that good, and acceptable, and perfect, will of God.

Basically, it is saying, you renew your mind (soul) You is not your mind(soul), because you is renewing the mind(soul). **You is your spirit.**

**If you feed your spirit, your spirit will be strong** and your spirit will control your body and soul(mind).

**If you do not feed your spirit, your spirit will be weak** and your body and soul(mind) will control you.

**You want your spirit fed by the Word** to control your body and soul(mind).

HEBREWS 4:12

> For the Word of God is quick, and powerful, and sharper than a two-edged sword, piercing even to the dividing asunder of soul and spirit, and of joints and marrow, and is a discerner of the thoughts and intents of the heart.

**How do we know if a thought we have is something we just made up or from God?** God speaks to us in our spirit. We have thoughts in our mind(soul). The spirit and soul are inter-connected.

This verse tells us the Word of God divides between soul and spirit. The Word of God is a discerner of the thoughts and intents of the heart. For our thoughts to be of God, they must line up with the Word of God. If our thoughts do not line up with the Word of God, they are simply our thoughts.

READ YOUR BIBLE EVERY DAY

I recommend that you start reading the Bible in the fourth book of the New Testament—**THE GOSPEL OF JOHN.** Let's say you read one chapter per day. One or two scriptures will stand out to you. **THIS IS GOD SPEAKING TO YOU.** This is the main way that God speaks to me.

After the Gospel of John read the rest of the New Testament except the Book of Revelation. Then read the Old Testament starting in Genesis. **Read the Book of Revelation last.** In the Book of Revelation there is a lot of signs and symbols. It will help you to understand the Book of Revelation, if you read the rest of the Bible first. It is important that you read the Book of Revelation. I have taught the entire Book of Revelation. I broke it down into 94 sessions.

(Go to: www.youtube.com Search: JOHNLV John L Vignes Revelation Bible Study)

**I CHALLENGE YOU TO READ THE ENTIRE BIBLE.** Set a goal of pages per day that is reasonable for you. **MY GOAL IS TO READ THROUGH THE BIBLE EVERY YEAR.** I try to read ten pages per day. Do I miss a day now and then? Yes. If you miss a day, don't try to make it up. Just start reading where you left off the next day. If you do this faithfully you will read through the entire Bible.

**Be encouraged.** At first it may be hard to read and understand the Bible. It was for me. Why? I had no background in the Bible. This happened to me. I was an A student as an undergraduate. In my first quarter in graduate school, I had to take biochemistry.

**I got an F on my first test!** I was confused. I couldn't understand anything. I studied, and studied, and studied. On my next test I got a C. I kept studying until one day it all fell into place. Why? I finally had enough background in biochemistry to understand what I was reading and being taught. I actually became a Teaching Assistant in a large biochemistry class. I promise you, if you keep reading and studying the Bible it will all become easier and easier. **Don't give up!** Ask God to help you. **The only person God can't work with is someone who gives up.**

## IMPORTANT BIBLE QUOTES BY JIMMY SWAGGART FOUND IN HIS EXPOSITOR'S STUDY BIBLE

**If we ignore the Bible,** we will lose our love for God.

**If we love the Bible,** we will love God.

**When all else fails,** read the instruction manual for humans (The Bible).

**For you to know the Bible,** is the single most important thing you can ever do.

**God's Word is tried if fire,** it has stood all tests.

**God's Word has never failed** those who have pleaded it's Promises and met it's terms before it's Author, God.

**The comfort that every soul needs** can only be derived from the Bible.

**God will always give bread** to a hungry heart.

**No Bible!** No freedom! **Little Bible!** Little freedom! **Much Bible!** Much freedom!

I encourage you to watch SonLife TV. (www.sonlifetv.com)

II TIMOTHY 2:15

**Study** to show yourself **approved unto God,**
**A workman** who needs not to be ashamed,
**rightly dividing the Word of Truth.**

# REACH OUT TO GOD WITH YOUR SPIRIT

THERE ARE THREE WAYS PEOPLE TRY TO REACH OUT TO GOD.

**Some people try to reach out to God through their physical senses.** Our physical senses are what we see, hear, taste, smell, and touch (feel). My physical body is always hungry. If I gave in to the physical sense of hunger every time, I would weigh 1000 lbs. Do I want to base my eternal future on my physical senses? No! **God is a Spirit and we must reach out to God with our spirit.**

**Some people try to reach out to God intellectually with their soul (Mind).** This is how Nicodemus tried to reach out to God, intellectually with his mind. He thought he had God figured out, but Jesus said Nicodemus you must be born again. We cannot figure out everything about God. It is impossible. For instance, where did God come from? Do I want to base my eternal future on my intellect? No! **God is a Spirit and we must reach out to God with our spirits.**

Because God is a spirit, we must reach out to God with our spirit, our heart, or inner-most being. **Being born again is when my spirit comes back into fellowship with God the Spirit. To be born again I must reach out to God with my spirit.**

## WHY DON'T PEOPLE REACH OUT TO GOD WITH THEIR SPIRIT

## II CORINTHIANS 4:3-4

> 3 **But if our Gospel be hid, it is hid to them who are lost:**
>
> 4 **In whom the god of this world** (Satan) **has blinded the minds of them which believe not,** lest the light of the Glorious Gospel of Christ, Who is the Image of God, should shine unto them.

**If you are not saved, if you are not born again,** Satan (the Devil) has blinded your mind? Why? He doesn't want you to hear the Gospel. He doesn't want you to understand the Word. Why? He doesn't want you to be born again. Satan hates God. The biggest way for Satan to hurt God is if he can stop you from being born again.

## HOW DOES SATAN BLIND OUR MINDS?

He tells us lies so we doubt God or so we won't believe there is a God. Satan told me two big lies to keep me from coming to God.

**GOD KILLED HIS SON JESUS ON THE CROSS.** The sixth Commandment is **thou shall not kill.** Satan asked me, "How can you believe in a God who would break His own Commandment and kill His own Son?" I did not realize that Jesus willingly gave His Life on the Cross for me:

GALATIANS 2:20

> I am Crucified with Christ: nevertheless I live; yet not I, but Christ lives in me: and the life which I now live in the flesh I live by the Faith of the Son of God, who loved me, **and gave Himself for me.**

**JOHN, YOU'RE A GOOD PERSON.** I agreed with Satan. I thought I was a good person. I worked hard. I studied hard. I tried to love and help people.

I thought God would think I was a good person and if my good outweighed my bad, I would go to Heaven. **I was wrong.** The Bible told me I was not a good person.

ROMAN 6:23

> **For all have sinned**, and have come short of the Glory of God.

ISAIAH 64:6

> But we are all an unclean thing, **but our righteousnesses are as filthy rags** ........

ECCLESIASTES 7:20

> For there is not a just (**righteous**) man upon the earth, **who does good, and sins not.**

JEREMIAH 17:9

> The heart is deceitful above all things, and **desperately wicked:** who can know it.

In my eyes, I thought I was a good person. Maybe in the eyes of the world, I was a good person.

However, in God's eyes I was not a good person. **I was a bad person. My heart was desperately wicked. I needed Jesus.**

# GOD'S MIRROR— THE TEN COMMANDMENTS

I love the Ten Commandments. I have really studied the Ten Commandments. I wrote a tract on the Ten Commandments.

**Many people say they "cannot communicate with God" or they "cannot hear God." However, God has given us a direct communication—the Ten Commandments.** When God gave the Ten Commandments, He did not have a man speak for Him—**God spoke.** He did not have a man write for Him—**God wrote them with His own finger on tablets of stone.** They were simple, clear, and direct so we could understand and follow them.

**The Ten Commandments were very important to God.** They were stored in the Ark of the Covenant, which was stored in the Tabernacle in the Holy of Holies. The people had to cleanse themselves before they came to Mount Sinai where they would meet

God and receive his commandments. Do you prepare your heart to receive God?

Moses brought the people forth to meet God. God descended on the mountain in fire. There was thunder and lightning. The mountain shook and smoke ascended from it. A trumpet blew louder and louder. **Then God Spoke.**

**Wouldn't that get you attention?** You would probably tremble and throw yourself face down in the dirt. **You would not dare to break even one of His commandments. You would not question if there was a God.** You would know there is a God and give Him the reverence, honor, and respect due Him.

**The Ten Commandments were important to God. If they are important to God, shouldn't they be important to us?** Some say we are now living in the Day of Grace and we no longer have to follow the commandments. This is false. Jesus used the commandments when He spoke to the rich, young ruler (Matthew 19:16-26). We are instructed to obey the commandments in the New Testament.

I JOHN 5:3

> For this is the love of God, **that we keep His commandments:** and His commandments are not grievous.

It cannot be clearer than this. **We must keep God's commandments.**

# WE HAVE BROKEN EVERY COMMANDMENT

Do you know we have broken everyone of **God's Ten Commandments**? I have, so I am not judging you. I am only going to go through three of the commandments to show this is true.

**Commandment 9—You shall not bear false witness.** This means that you cannot lie. We do not take lying very seriously, but God does.

REVELATION 21:8

> But the fearful, and unbelieving, and the abominable, and murderers, and whoremongers, and sorcerers, and idolaters, **and all liars** shall have their part in the lake which burns with fire and brimstone: which is the second death.

Have you ever told a lie? What do you call someone that has told a lie? A liar. **In God's eyes, what are you? A liar.**

**Commandment 7—You shall not commit adultery.** Most of us would say we have never committed adultery. Any sex outside of marriage is adultery. The Bible teaches marriage is between a man and a woman. Jesus indicated that if we lust in our hearts for another, we have committed adultery.

MATTHEW 5:27-28

> 27 You have heard that it was said by them of old time, **You shall not commit adultery.**
>
> 28 But I say unto you, That whosoever looks on a woman to lust after her **has committed adultery with her already in his heart.**

All of us have lusted for another. Pornography causes us to lust. Lust is adultery. What do you call someone who has committed adultery? An adulterer. **In God's eyes, what are you? An adulterer.**

**COMMANDMENT 6—You shall not kill.** Most of us would say we have never killed anyone. What does the Bible say? The Bible warns us that if we hate someone, we are murders.

## I JOHN 3:15

> **Whosoever hates his brother is a murderer:** and you know that **no murderer has eternal life abiding in him.**

If you hate someone in your heart even for a moment, what are you? A murderer. **In God's eyes, what are you? A murderer.**

I have shown in just three commandments that you are a liar, an adulterer, and a murderer. **Considering this, how do you expect to get into Heaven?** You must be born again.

The Ten Commandments have no power to save us. The Ten Commandments show us we have sinned and we need Jesus. **I love the Ten Commandments because they showed me my sin and my need for Jesus.** When I see how much I have been forgiven, I love Jesus more and more. The Ten Commandments are no longer grievous to me. I desire to obey the commandments because I love Jesus. Jesus helps me obey the commandments.

# YOU MUST BE BORN AGAIN

Do you see your sins? You will not get anywhere with Jesus **until you see the real you.** Not the person you see, **the real you.** Not the person others see, **the real you.** Do you see your need for Jesus? **You must be born again.**

JOHN 3:5

> Jesus answered, Verily, verily, I say unto you, **except a man be born of water and of the Spirit,** he cannot enter into the Kingdom of God.

Each one of us must be born of water and of the Spirit.

**Born of water** refers to our physical birth.

**Born of the Spirit** refers to being born again.

## HOW DO I BECOME BORN AGAIN?

### ROMANS 10:9-10

> 9 But if **you shall confess with your mouth the Lord Jesus,** and shall **believe in your heart** that God has raised Him from the dead, **you shall be saved** (**born again**).
>
> 10 For with the heart **man believes unto righteousness**; and with the mouth **confession is made unto salvation.**

If you will put your faith and trust in Jesus, ask Him to forgive your sins, believe God raised Him from the dead, and invite Jesus into your life as your Lord and Savior; you will be saved. The righteousness of Christ will be given to you. **His righteousness is pure, holy and perfect. It is the only righteousness God will accept.** God will not accept your self-righteousness.

**You must keep your faith in Jesus and what he did at the Cross at all times, and nothing else.** Don't put your faith in your good works, how much you go to church, how much you read your Bible, religious ceremonies (baptism, confirmation, or communion) or anything else. You must keep your faith in Jesus at all times. I do not put my faith in myself, because I fail. **I put my faith in Jesus, because He never fails.** If you put your faith in Jesus, the Holy Spirit will work in your heart and life to bring you victory over your sins. You will become more and more Christ-like every day.

## WHEN YOU ARE BORN AGAIN, GOD WILL GIVE YOU A NEW HEART

### EZEKIEL 11:19-20

> 19 And I will give them one heart, and I will put a new spirit within you; and **I will take the stony heart out of their flesh, and will give them an heart of flesh.**
>
> 20 That they may walk in My Statutes, and keep My Ordinances, and do them: **and they shall be my people, and I will be their God.**

## MY LIFE WITH JESUS HAS GONE THROUGH FOUR STAGES

### 1. Slave

When I first came to Christ, I was a slave. I did not want to pray, read my Bible, and go to church. I wanted to drink, party, and chase girls. However, I started doing these things out of obedience to God.

**2. Disciple**

I started praying, reading my Bible, and going to church. Guess what happened? God did some miracles for me. I have a scientific background. My attitude was always, prove it to me. God did. Then I knew the Bible was true. The Bible became alive and exciting to me. I am a disciple to this day. I spend most of my time reading and studying the Word of God.

**3. Friend**

Eventually I become friends with Jesus. I share Jesus with everyone I can, not because I have to, but because Jesus is my friend. I wrote this book to share Jesus because he is my friend. I want everyone to know my friend Jesus and go to Heaven.

**4. One**

My relationship with Jesus got so good that we became one—just like a husband and wife should be one. Every day I look for good things I can do for

Jesus, and I believe Jesus looks for good things He can do for me.

If I sin, I break my relationship with Jesus and I go back to being a slave. The good thing is I can confess my sin and Jesus is faithful and just to forgive me. My relationship then goes right back to being one with Jesus.

## IF YOU WOULD LIKE TO ACCEPT JESUS AND BE BORN AGAIN, PLEASE PRAY THIS PRAYER.

**Father**, I come to you in the **precious name of Jesus.**

**Jesus**, I ask you to **forgive my sins.**

**I believe God** raised you **from the dead.**

**I invite** you into my **heart** as **my Lord and Savior.**

**I do not put my faith** in anything I do.

**I put my faith** in you Jesus and what you did at the Cross.

**I ask you for the gift of eternal life**, I receive it, and I thank you for it.

**Jesus,** please deliver me from all my sins and **be Lord of my life.**

# TO UNDERSTAND THE BIBLE, YOU MUST UNDERSTAND THE CROSS

**When I am speaking of the Cross, I mean putting my faith in Jesus and what He did at the Cross.** I am writing this book in March 2022. I have been saved for **44 years.** To get saved I had to recognize my sin, ask God to forgive my sins, ask him to be the Lord of my life, and put my faith in Jesus and what He did at the Cross. I started reading my Bible right away. **I understood the Cross for my salvation, but I did not understand the Cross for sanctification (becoming more Christ- Like every day) or living a victorious Christian Life.**

**I did not see the Cross in the Bible** unless the actual word Cross was used. However, I have found that the Cross runs through the entire Bible. All of the Sacrifices, the Passover, and all of the Jewish Feast Days point to the Cross. Every Sacred Vessel in the Temple and the Temple itself points to the Cross. In the New Testament when we take communion, we drink the wine or grape juice (**Jesus said remember me**), when we eat the bread (**Jesus said remember me**). **Communion and Water Baptism** point to the Cross. In Revelation the word **Lamb** is used over and over. The Bible says to be saved our name must be written in **The Lamb's Book of Life.** The word **Lamb** points to the Cross.

To live a victorious Christian life we must always keep our faith in Jesus and what He did at the Cross.

I learned most of what I know about the Cross from Pastor Jimmy Swaggart in his excellent Expositor's Study Bible, Commentaries, and SonLife TV (www.sonlifetv.com). Thank you Pastor Jimmy.

# BE CAREFUL WHAT YOU LISTEN TO OR READ

## I CORINTHIANS 1:17-18

17 For Christ sent me, not to baptize, **but to preach the Gospel:** not with the wisdom of words, **lest the Cross of Christ should be made of none effect.**

18 **For the preaching of the Cross** is to them who perish foolishness; but unto us who are saved **it is the Power of God.**

Paul was sent to preach the Gospel. What is the Gospel? Many believe the Gospel is the Good News that God wants everyone to be rich, famous, and never have a problem. **No! No! No!** This is not the Gospel. The Gospel is Jesus came, He died on the Cross for our sins, and He rose again. This is the Good News. This is the best news any of us can receive. Paul was not to preach with the wisdom of words (The words of men). Why? It could make the Cross of none effect. If Paul preached with the words of men it could negate to many, everything Jesus did on the Cross. If what someone is preaching and teaching minimizes the Cross (Jesus and what He did on the Cross), it is false. **Why was Paul to preach the Cross?** The preaching of the Cross **is the Power of God.**

## WHERE DOES THE POWER COME FROM?

ROMANS 8:2

> For the **Law of the Spirit of Life in Christ Jesus** has set me free from the **Law of Sin and Death.**

These are the two greatest laws in the universe. The Law of Sin and Death is the law everyone who is not saved is under. If they do not accept Christ they will sin, and sin and sin. Eventually they will die and go to hell. There is only one law that is greater than the Law of Sin and Death, that is the Law of the Spirit of Life in Christ Jesus. **The Spirit of Life** is the Holy Spirit.

Notice it says the Law of the Spirit of Life **is in Christ Jesus.** This means that for the Holy Spirit to work in our lives **we must keep our faith in Jesus and what He did at the Cross.** If we focus our faith in any other direction, it will hinder or limit the work of the Holy Spirit in our lives. **The Holy Spirit does not work outside the Cross.**

I do not have the power to save, heal, or deliver anyone; but the Holy Spirit does. If you read all the Promises in the New Testament, it says that every Promise comes through, by, and in Christ Jesus. This means that every **blessing we have from God** comes through our faith in Jesus and what He did at the Cross. **Most people do not see those small, but extremely important, words.**

**Paul was one of the most powerful men of God that ever lived?** Why? He Preached the Cross.

## I CORINTHIANS 12:2

> For I determined not to know anything among you, **save Jesus Christ, and Him Crucified.**

Where did Paul focus his faith? In Jesus, not just Jesus; but in Jesus Christ and Him Crucified. **You cannot separate Jesus from His Cross and you cannot separate the Cross from Jesus.**

## I CORINTHIANS 1:23

**But we preach Christ Crucified.....**

What did they preach? **WE PREACH CHRIST CRUCIFIED! It says we.** Who is we? It is not just the Apostle Paul preaching the Cross. It was we. This is what the Apostles, Elders, Preachers, Teachers, Evangelists, and Church Leaders in the Book of Acts preached. **They preached Christ Crucified.** This is why the church was born in such power. **They preached Christ Crucified.**

**If your faith is not focused in Jesus and what he did at the Cross as you read this book,** I have failed you and I am sorry.

## WHAT FOCUSING ON THE CROSS HAS DONE FOR ME

**THIS IS WHAT FOCUSING MY FAITH ON JESUS AND WHAT HE DID AT THE CROSS HAS DONE FOR ME.** It was like being born again-again. Now **the LOVE AND POWER OF GOD FLOWS THROUGH ME.** I no longer struggle in the flesh as much. The Holy Spirit has given me the power to overcome my sins. I could not do it without the power of the Holy Spirit. God has done miracle after miracle for me. **God has blessed me over and over.**

### GOD HAS DEALT WITH MY PRIDE

Do you know that pride is the number one sin that God hates the most (Proverbs 6:16-19)? Why? Our pride keeps us from admitting our need for Jesus. We think we can do it all on our own. How is that working for you? You need the power of the Holy Spirit to work in you. Since I've focused my faith on the Cross:

1. I've realized it is about Him, and not me. This took care of my pride.
2. I've realized the great price Jesus paid for my sins; this makes me grateful.
3. I've realized how sinful I was and that my sin was destroying me, this makes me thankful.
4. I realize how hateful I was toward Jesus, yet He died on the Cross for me. This is **Grace.** I did not deserve the good things Jesus has done for me. This makes me love Jesus more and more.
5. I realize the great value God placed on me. He sent His only Son (**Jesus**) to die on the Cross for me. **He did not condemn me—He valued me!**

**When my faith has been in the Cross, THE BIBLE HAS COME ALIVE TO ME.** It has opened up the Bible to me. It has increased my understanding of the Bible and strengthened my faith. **TO UNDERSTAND THE BIBLE, YOU MUST UNDERSTAND THE CROSS.** I now preach and teach the Cross. I encourage you to learn from me.

**Please share this book with everyone you can. Please listen to and share my Messages on the Cross on my YouTube Channel—John for Jesus.** Search John Vignes Sermons on YouTube.

# A CALL TO ACTION

Jesus told us to follow Him and he would make us "**Fishers of Men.**" To catch fish, you have to go fishing. You have to put bait on the hook and cast it into the water. **Use this book** as the bait on your hook and cast it into the water (**Give it to the lost**).

## IT IS NOT ENOUGH TO JUST PRAY, YOU MUST GO FISHING

**This is a true story.** There was a woman's prayer group that met every week for years. Every week they prayed for a woman next door who was a prostitute. **Despite years of praying, this woman did not get saved.**

**One day an Evangelist preached to the prayer group.** After his message the prayer group told him about the prostitute next door that they had prayed for year after year. The Evangelist asked, "**Did you**

**ever share Jesus with her?"** They had to say **no**. The Evangelist told them to **go share Jesus** with her. They did and she got saved.

Many of us have prayed for years and years for our lost family, friends, loves ones, and people we work with. They have not gotten saved. **It is not enough just to pray, you must share Jesus with them.**

## WE ARE TO GO OUT INTO ALL THE WORLD

ACTS 1:8

> But you **shall receive power**, after that the **Holy Spirit is come upon you:** and you shall be witnesses unto me both in Jerusalem, and in all Judea, and in Samaria, and **unto the uttermost part of the earth.**

**We are to share Jesus with the world.** This does not mean we have to pack up our belongings and go to another country as a Missionary. This means we must **share Jesus with our personal world.** Our personal world is everyone we meet on our journey through life. **Evangelism is not just for Pastors and Evangelists, it is for everyone.** As we go out and share Jesus the Holy Spirit will empower us.

## JESUS NEEDS WORKERS—SOWERS AND REAPERS

## JOHN 4:35-38

35 Say not ye, there are four months, and then cometh harvest? Behold, I say unto you, lift up your eyes, and look on the fields: for they are white **already to harvest.**

36 And He who reaps receives wages, **and gathers fruit unto eternal life:** that both he who sows and he who reaps may rejoice together.

37 And herein is that saying true, one **sows** and another **reaps.**

38 I sent you to reap whereon you bestowed no labor: other men labored, and you have entered into their labors.

**There are two kinds of workers—sowers and reapers.**
**What if no one sows?**
**What if no one reaps?**
**We must go into the Harvest Field of the Lord.**

**In 2005 I published my first tract—The Stain of Sin.** Osterhus Publishing House in Minneapolis, Minnesota printed my tract. I was speaking with someone at Osterhus Publishing. They told me. "John, we used to sell thousands and thousands of tracts here in Minneapolis and St. Paul, now we hardly sell any." **This broke my heart.** The reason America and the World are turning from God is **very few Christians are sharing Jesus.** Do you think that if we do not share Jesus, He will say to us "**well done faithful servant?**" I don't think so.

## SOW TRACTS AND BOOKS

This is some information I found in a book by C. S. Lovett—Teach Witnessing, The Ladder Method. Tract (or books). "Tracts are like bullets. They strike the target with terrific impact. They are like verbal pellets, which slam into a man's spirit and once lodged, are not easy to remove. A victim can run, but he cannot escape an idea that has fixed itself in his understanding. As these words keep coming back, they act like a thorn to his conscience. And thorns, if not removed, fester and cause great pain. More than one man has felt the continued sting of God's printed invitation once it found its way to his soul."

**The reason I hand out books or tracts** is to sow a **Gospel Seed** in a person's heart so the **Holy Spirit can work on that seed to bring salvation.** (**John L Vignes**)

I CORINTHIANS 3:7

> So, neither is he who plants anything, neither he who waters; **but God who gives the increase.**

# ACTION FROM THE PAST

## ECCLESIASTES 11:6

In the morning **sow your seed**, and it the evening **withhold not your hand:** for you know not whether shall prosper, either this or that, or whether they both shall be alike good.

## FACTS ABOUT TRACTS OR BOOKS

**God uses them.** He used a tract to save the great missionary **Hudson Taylor.**

**C. H. Spurgeon** "When preaching and private talk are not available, you need to have a tract ready ... get good striking tracts, or none at all. But a touching gospel tract may be the seed of eternal life. Therefore, **do not go out without your tracts.**"

**George Whitefield** read one called, "**The Life of God in the Soul of a Man,**" he said, "God showed me I must be born again or be damned." He went on to pray, "**Lord if I am not a Christian, or if I am not a real one, for Jesus Christ's sake show me what Christianity is, that I not be damned at last!**" Then in his journal tells us "from that moment...did I know I must become a new creature," Whitefield Journals, p52.

**William Penn** wrote a single religious tract that freed a total of 12,000 Quakers imprisoned for Christ's sake.

**John Wesley** organized 160 tract distributors in 1757 which literally reformed the Lord's Day habits of the entire city of London.

**Martin Luther** wrote more than one tract, booklet, or book for every working week of his entire life.

**D. L. Moody** began his very fruitful evangelistic ministry in Chicago by the simple act of distributing tracts to Great Lake seamen.

Almost every mission field was opened by missionaries who first used tracts to win heathen to Christ.

Every phase of the **Protestant Reformation** was preceded by immense tract efforts that almost "**turned the world upside down.**"

**Precious cargo on the Mayflower** included Pastor John Robinson's tracts.

The son of one of the chiefs of Burdwain, India was converted by a single tract. He was instrumental in winning 1,500 natives to Christ!

Someone once gave "**The Inspiration of the Bible**" to four infidels at different times. All four were saved and became preachers of the Gospel.

Years ago, a lady gave a leaflet to two actors. One got saved, **Dr George Lorimer**, and became Pastor of Tremont Baptist Temple in Boston. Through his influence, **Dr. Russell H. Conwell** was led into the ministry.

A young Frenchman, wounded at the siege of Saint Quentin, was languishing on his hospital bed when a tract laying on the table caught his eyes. He read it and was saved. A monument of that man, standing with a Bible in his hand, may be seen before the Church of the Consistory in Paris. He was **Admiral Coligny**, the leader of the **Reformation in France.** The tract was read by his nurse, who placed it in the hands of **Lady Abbess** and she was saved. **Lady Abbess** fled from France to the Palatinate where she met a young Hollander and became his wife. The influence she had upon that man reacted upon **the whole continent of Europe for he was William of Orange, who became the champion of liberty and of Protestantism in the Netherlands.**

**Dr. Oswald J. Smith** said, "The only way to carry out the Great Commission will be by means of the printed page."

**Please use this book** (**What Does it Mean to Be Born Again?**) to go fishing for the Lord.

## SOME PLACES TO FISH

- Give them to family, friends, loved ones and people you work with.
- Hand them out at fairs, swap meets, flea markets, rodeos, fourth of July Celebrations, and restaurants (anywhere people gather).
- Hand them out at hospitals to patients when you visit them. Share them with the Hospital Chaplains.
- Hand them out in prisons and share them with Prison Chaplains.
- Give them to people in drug and alcohol treatment programs.
- Share them with College Christian groups and students.
- Write a Christmas letter and send this book out as a gift.
- If you own a business give them to your customers and employees. Leave a supply out

somewhere in your business. Leave them out on retail counters.

- Give them to your Pastors or Church Leaders.
- Hand them out in convenience stores where you buy gas.
- Leave them in your hotel rooms.
- Give or send them to all the unsaved people you pray for.

PUT THIS BOOK IN THE HANDS OF EVERY SOUL WINNER YOU KNOW. THEY HAVE A PASSION FOR THE LOST.

**God, I pray you will use this book (What Does it Mean to Be Born Again?) to win millions to Christ. Raise up an army of soul winners all over the world. Give us divine appointments. Guide us where to give and how to use this book.**

**Amen.**

Manufactured by Amazon.ca
Bolton, ON

26534053R00046